Fatal

ALSO BY KIMBERLY JOHNSON

POETRY

Uncommon Prayer

A Metaphorical God

Leviathan with a Hook

Before the Door of God: An Anthology of Devotional Poetry
(co-edited with Jay Hopler)

POETRY IN TRANSLATION

Theogony and Works and Days by Hesiod

The Georgics: A Poem of the Land by Virgil

LITERARY CRITICISM

Made Flesh: Sacrament and Poetics in Post-Reformation England

Fatal

Kimberly Johnson

A Karen & Michael Braziller Book
PERSEA BOOKS / NEW YORK

Persea Books, Inc.
90 Broad Street
New York, NY 10004

LCCN: 2022930431

Designed by Rita Lascaro
Manufactured in the United States of America.

In memory of.

Contents

death cannot harm me
more than you have harmed me,
my beloved life.

—Louise Glück, "October"

FALL, UNSPECIFIED (W19)

WORK TABLE I. DEATHS FROM EACH CAUSE, BY 5-YEAR AGE
GROUPS: UNITED STATES, 2001

All ages -------- 7,660
Under 1 year---- 8
1-4 years------- 4
5-9 years------- 6
10-14 years----- 8
15-19 years----- 11
20-24 years----- 22
25-29 years----- 23
30-34 years----- 41
35-39 years----- 77
40-44 years----- 143
45-49 years----- 179
50-54 years----- 201
55-59 years----- 178
60-64 years----- 236
65-69 years----- 345
70-74 years----- 532
75-79 years----- 993
80-84 years----- 1,438
85-89 years----- 1,561
90-94 years----- 1,124
95-99 years----- 446
100 yrs & over--- 82
Notstated-------- 2

U.S. ACTUARIAL TABLES/CENTERS FOR DISEASE CONTROL

FOR CAUSE-OF-DEATH CODES, SEE HTTP://WWW.CDC.GOV/NCHS
AND REFER TO "TECHNICAL APPENDIX FROM VITAL STATISTICS
OF THE UNITED STATES: MORTALITY, 2001"

CAUSE OF DEATH BASED ON THE TENTH REVISION,
INTERNATIONAL CLASSIFICATION OF DISEASES

Fall

                    Dear One, I've come home
To aftermath: unseasonable snow
Has snapped the apple tree in half, branches
Cracked, scattered apples a thousand damaged
Hearts across the yard, a windfall already
Spoiling. I've read the news: daily outrages
Against the human, ruin in triage,
Against which shocks what is the fall of a tree?,
My life so small and common I am ashamed
To feel it as a risk. And yet—.
                             All my care
Sudden uprooted and open to weather,
Dumbfound I at my unhomely door remain,
Keyring in my fist a plug of cordite,
Lock a latent spark, whole world ready to ignite.

FALLOPIAN TUBE (C57.0)

WORK TABLE I. DEATHS FROM EACH CAUSE, BY 5-YEAR AGE
GROUPS: UNITED STATES, 2001

All ages -------- 172
Under 1 year-----
1-4   years-------
5-9   years-------
10-14 years-----
15-19 years-----
20-24 years-----
25-29 years-----
30-34 years-----
35-39 years-----
40-44 years-----   1
45-49 years-----
50-54 years-----   16
55-59 years-----   19
60-64 years-----   16
65-69 years-----   21
70-74 years-----   36
75-79 years-----   25
80-84 years-----   18
85-89 years-----   8
90-94 years-----   4
95-99 years-----   1
100 yrs & over---
Notstated--------

U.S. ACTUARIAL TABLES/CENTERS FOR DISEASE CONTROL

FOR CAUSE-OF-DEATH CODES, SEE HTTP://WWW.CDC.GOV/NCHS
AND REFER TO "TECHNICAL APPENDIX FROM VITAL STATISTICS
OF THE UNITED STATES: MORTALITY, 2001"

CAUSE OF DEATH BASED ON THE TENTH REVISION,
INTERNATIONAL CLASSIFICATION OF DISEASES

Familial

Automatic, planless,
My father startled from his roadside piss

Kicks gun to shoulder cranks shell to chamber
Knocks the buck down.
His jeans bag at his ankle.

My orange plastic vest crackles in the wind.
I am ten.
We are ten miles out from camp,

Dirtbike half-slung off the mud-rutted road
While at our feet
The unintended four-point

Sinks into the redly melting snow. Masterly
Our butchery:
Quick jugulation, bloodless slice

Down the center line as I hold the hind legs wide,
The tugs that empty
Throat and heart, guts and sex

Onto the ground for coyotes. Like lords I think
Our progress
Back to camp, the carcass

Upright on the motorcycle seat, hooves
Roped to pedal
And handlebar, head half-severed

Lolling antlers back onto my father's shoulder
        While I, snugged
        Into its vertical gash, throttle

Down the mountain. I am redhanded, wind-raw
        And triumphal.
        I am my father's son.

Farrow

Full in the fat wallow of me,
        Superfluity
    Even to the marrow—

Blood plumping along in a red swell
        Of venules
    Blushing my most unabashed

Skinpatches: nosetip, earlobe, wristshallow. O
        This mother
    Is a crush of too-muchness,

A malady of my baffled self awash.
        Accomplished
    Finally the days, will I find

My bones I lost?, will my sharps and edges
        Hedge this fleshy
    Habit I've made of excess?

Already my heartracing startles
        In another's
    Twitches, my dinner hiccups

Another's diaphragm. Already and almost
        I swear I feel
    The protein creep of me, cell

By splitting cell, into another's life.
        My mother-grief
    Sorrows not for the heart-close one

I'll lose from me at my delivery
            But for my own
        Soul overboiling, unbound, bound

To a stranger's groans, undone by his hurts
            And remorses
        To the third and fourth

Generations. What I'm birthing is my own
            Diffusion.
        Never again mere. Never again my own.

Farthingale

Lo my pennyworth of windblown,
                    Hurricane
          Of lash and whalebone,

How often I've fastened its billows
                    About me,
          Sashed beneath furbelows.

Tight cinches the corset, tighter the stays,
                    Smooth and tight
          For the bodice's lacings,

But my underpinnings upgust
                    From ankle
          To thigh to the untrussed

Cyclonic eye of me. I'm the low-
                    Pressure system
          Sinking the barometer,

The microburst havocking
                    The weathercock,
          While I battened down to placid

Seem, as a white-glove Sunday
                    In June.
          Like all tempests I say

Hallelujah for the cage,
                    The isobars,
          The wickerwork and cartilage

Within whose strictures wildness can wind
        Itself up
      To the shape of its binding.

It's the lid sets the teakettle rocking
        At the boil,
      The shell's song the gunpowder sings.

Faster

The first chariot race took place the day
       The second chariot
        Rolled from the wheelwright's workshop.

Spooked horses flared at the unfamiliar
       Wheelgrind in gravel,
        The spoked hub's squeal around its axle,

The hitchpole's sudden itch against the flanks.
       The drivers twitched
        Leathers and fidgeted their whips,

Each eyeing sidelong his rival's rig. What,
       In those unbreathing
        Heartbeats before the start,

Did they brace to outrun? The nervy one
       In the next car?
        Or a steadier champion,

Implacable, whose pace unslacking pressed
       Ever just behind,
        In hoofbeats and hot breath.

The third charioteer slicked back his hair
       And greased his axle-
        Tree. The fourth affixed

Tailfins and a spoiler. Turbocharger.
       Turbine. The next
        And next, and every newest fangle surges

Further toward that unreachable
        Where deathless
      On every tongue fame flutters

Like a checkered flag. We charioteers
        Are only brief-
      Ly faster than our fears.

FATIGUE (G93.3)

WORK TABLE I. DEATHS FROM EACH CAUSE, BY 5-YEAR AGE
GROUPS: UNITED STATES, 2001

All ages --------	3
Under 1 year-----	
1-4 years-------	
5-9 years-------	
10-14 years-----	
15-19 years-----	
20-24 years-----	
25-29 years-----	
30-34 years-----	
35-39 years-----	
40-44 years-----	
45-49 years-----	
50-54 years-----	
55-59 years-----	
60-64 years-----	
65-69 years-----	
70-74 years-----	
75-79 years-----	2
80-84 years-----	1
85-89 years-----	
90-94 years-----	
95-99 years-----	
100 yrs & over---	
Not stated-------	

U.S. ACTUARIAL TABLES/CENTERS FOR DISEASE CONTROL

FOR CAUSE-OF-DEATH CODES, SEE HTTP://WWW.CDC.GOV/NCHS
AND REFER TO "TECHNICAL APPENDIX FROM VITAL STATISTICS
OF THE UNITED STATES: MORTALITY, 2001"

CAUSE OF DEATH BASED ON THE TENTH REVISION,
INTERNATIONAL CLASSIFICATION OF DISEASES

Female

Locker-room truant in a locked stall
                    Through study hall
              Hiding, hand-stifling her cries,

A girl wide-eyes the unimagined smear
                    Of blood rusting
              Her fingertips. Secret, quaint horror.

Some betrayal of the flesh has left her
                    Vulnerable,
              Her blithe pellmell

Redefining to this singularity. But no.
                    She is smarter
              Than her body. She will starve

This woman out, she will run and outrun
                    The turncoat moon.
              She will firesale down

To a shoestring inventory: *item*:
                    Two eyes, indifferent
              Blue; *item*: brain and brainstem;

Item: one mouth, tightened like a screwcap
                    On the business end
              Of the pipebomb she's just become.

Fever

1.

The sky is shut. No bright lines

Against the fading day, no wingtip lights
                    Attend us
            Companionably at midnight.

2.

My mother's eightieth birthday: masked,
        I sang
        My cheer across the grass. I asked

If she needed groceries, chalked a poem
        Onto her street.
        Hugged the air and then went home.

3.

but, Lord! how empty the streets are and melancholy, so many poor sick people. . . ; and so many sad stories overheard as I walk, every body talking of this dead, and that man sick, and so many in this place, and so many in that. And they tell me that, in Westminster, there is never a physician and but one apothecary left, all being dead; but that there are great hopes of a great decrease this week: God send it!

Samuel Pepys, 1665

4.

The air is shut. Those suspect molecules
            Skulk from lethal
        You to lethal me, our bronchioles

Defenseless in this novel wind. We shrink
            From touching, flinch
        Away from welcome and the rank

Vapor of good wishes. We are all made
            Ghosts together.

5.

And now I am my owne pale Empty Shade.

Lucy Hutchinson, c. 1664

6.

Forty days of doldrums like forty days of rain.
                    We each an ark
            Whose freight is moored uncertain

Off the coast of Venice. *Quarantino*
                        As they counted,
            A proof against contagion

Biblically drawn out. Our own becalmèd days
                    Lengthen past
            Their season; each held fast

We in our own rooms, we keep the windows
                    Sealed, we wouldn't know
            If some bird with a twig happened to show.

7.

Our dramas have become soliloquies.

8.

        Faraway
     My love, each passing day

Is felt as distance, space as long as time
         It takes to travel
     From ocean yours to desert mine

By imperiled car. You cannot fly.
        The sky
   Is shut.

9.

My ruinous anatomy

Donne called the keepsake scrawl he left
As consolation
When absence him his love bereft.

Here's my own packet of bedraggled words,
A paper
Airplane folded and released

Across the vast pandemic miles to land,
Perhaps the worse
For wear, into your hands.

FEVER OF UNKNOWN ORIGIN (R50)

WORK TABLE I. DEATHS FROM EACH CAUSE, BY 5-YEAR AGE
GROUPS: UNITED STATES, 2001

All ages --------	47
Under 1 year----	2
1-4 years-------	2
5-9 years-------	
10-14 years-----	
15-19 years-----	1
20-24 years-----	1
25-29 years-----	1
30-34 years-----	2
35-39 years-----	1
40-44 years-----	2
45-49 years-----	2
50-54 years-----	
55-59 years-----	
60-64 years-----	2
65-69 years-----	1
70-74 years-----	10
75-79 years-----	6
80-84 years-----	5
85-89 years-----	3
90-94 years-----	3
95-99 years-----	2
100 yrs & over---	1
Not stated-------	

U.S. ACTUARIAL TABLES/CENTERS FOR DISEASE CONTROL

FOR CAUSE-OF-DEATH CODES, SEE HTTP://WWW.CDC.GOV/NCHS
AND REFER TO "TECHNICAL APPENDIX FROM VITAL STATISTICS
OF THE UNITED STATES: MORTALITY, 2001"

CAUSE OF DEATH BASED ON THE TENTH REVISION,
INTERNATIONAL CLASSIFICATION OF DISEASES

F-hole

Run your thumb under the trembling
              String along
        The fretted neck, and back

The curve and burnish of the sounding board
              Then rim a fingertip
        Over and into the cutout lip,

Luthier, to the spruce's smooth expose.
              What the knife knows
        Is its own sweet progress

Through the woodgrain. What the woodgrain knows
              Will at last hum
        Through what passage the blade opens,

Released like a long sigh into the world's
              Unwitting ear.
        The whimsied engineer

Who first this flourish scribed aspired less
              To the nice math
        Of resonant frequencies

And pressure differentials than to the curl
              Shaving pale
        And warm into his palm,

The one whose whorls he longed to touch.
              What other love
        Can explain the plaintive

Timbre of this Cremonese fancy?:
                Unanswerable
        Strain through the finial's swell

To the hearing's inmost chamber. His error
                Of exchange
        To us as a heritage remains;

Belated even to our own fleet loves,
                We invent
        For every one an accident

To be tooled as a seal into anything
                We can hold.
        Thus, luthier, do you bring

Your knives to bed. Thus do you wear my ring.

FIBRILLATION AND FLUTTER (I49.0)

WORK TABLE I. DEATHS FROM EACH CAUSE, BY 5-YEAR AGE
GROUPS: UNITED STATES, 2001

All ages --------	1,406
Under 1 year----	
1-4 years-------	
5-9 years-------	1
10-14 years-----	3
15-19 years-----	5
20-24 years-----	3
25-29 years-----	8
30-34 years-----	12
35-39 years-----	15
40-44 years-----	29
45-49 years-----	65
50-54 years-----	72
55-59 years-----	103
60-64 years-----	120
65-69 years-----	143
70-74 years-----	158
75-79 years-----	226
80-84 years-----	188
85-89 years-----	156
90-94 years-----	80
95-99 years-----	19
100 yrs & over---	
Notstated--------	

U.S. ACTUARIAL TABLES/CENTERS FOR DISEASE CONTROL

FOR CAUSE-OF-DEATH CODES, SEE HTTP://WWW.CDC.GOV/NCHS
AND REFER TO "TECHNICAL APPENDIX FROM VITAL STATISTICS
OF THE UNITED STATES: MORTALITY, 2001"

CAUSE OF DEATH BASED ON THE TENTH REVISION,
INTERNATIONAL CLASSIFICATION OF DISEASES

Fidelity

Heaven-selvage, twilight eyelet opened
Through the wind-
Scrubbed drab at the ridgeline,

Splash of freshet nestled into stone,
What with bone-
Dry, blasted me have you to do?

Gentiana verna, do not intimate
Of spring,
Do not rouse the secret

Bee that waggles in my breast to honey
To your hue,
What have you to do with me?

Do with me, flash lapis lazuli
Swatched from the hem
Of some Flemish madonna,

What you will, O do you subsume me
In deepwater blue.
Do me cerulean through.

✿

But when you welkin me, whelm like a brigand,
Like the whole couloir's
A blue desire before whose force

My will must break. Blossom, will I break
Faith with this rough-
Cast, this cherished chaff,

This earthbound habit for your unearthly?,
Can I forsake
This my sure estate for your ec-

Stasies on spec, for your fathomless X?

Fifteen

[*Terrapin!*] [*Tentacle!*] In the atrium
                Brightness my sons'
        Delight presses so close

To the canvas the guard coughs a caution.
                The commotion
        Of wing and fang that is Bruegel's *Fall*

Of the Rebel Angels hangs like a trespass,
                [*Claw!*] [*Carapace!*]
        Like a curious cabinet

Had sex with a scavenger hunt. [*Salamander!*]
                Halfway headlong
        Down his hurtle one handles

In his demonic fist a fishbasket
                Finned with switches.
        Another faller fledges

Into swallowtail, the fleshy edges
                Of his lewdness
        Startled with butterfly finery.

A third [*Hurdy-gurdy!*] is girt with the garnet
                And sudden gold
        Wings of the lucifer bird,—

Every peculiar pursued to its foundering
          Is part something
     Else, [*Armadillo!*] [*Esquire!*]

As agog at itself as at an ambush
          Of angels. My angels,
     Half-plunged into each your own strangeness,

Gangly and almost in need of a shave,
          [*Amphibian!*]
     [*Astrolabe!*] as the transiting sun

Through the windowpane frames you momently still
          In your mutual
     Conclave of puzzle and name,

I observing can guess why the heavens
          Mustered, taking
     To trumpet and frantic buckler:

Some with swords would arrest that reverseless
          [*Pufferfish!*] fall,
     Holding fast their once familiars

By force. But see, in the ether—a flourish
          Of brasses, a mass
     Of seraphs suspended, weaponless.

I suppose those horns clarion not in discord
          But in blessing,
     A benediction on the dim,

Bewildered way ahead, which as yet
      They do not know,
   And so cannot regret.

FIREWORK DISCHARGE (W39)

WORK TABLE I. DEATHS FROM EACH CAUSE, BY 5-YEAR AGE
GROUPS: UNITED STATES, 2001

```
All ages --------        6
Under 1 year-----
1-4 years--------
5-9 years--------
10-14 years------
15-19 years------
20-24  years-----        2
25-29 years------
30-34  years-----        1
35-39  years-----        1
40-44 years------
45-49  years-----        1
50-54 years------
55-59  years-----        1
60-64 years------
65-69 years------
70-74 years------
75-79 years------
80-84 years------
85-89 years------
90-94 years------
95-99 years------
100 yrs & over---
Notstated--------
```

U.S. ACTUARIAL TABLES/CENTERS FOR DISEASE CONTROL

FOR CAUSE-OF-DEATH CODES, SEE HTTP://WWW.CDC.GOV/NCHS
AND REFER TO "TECHNICAL APPENDIX FROM VITAL STATISTICS
OF THE UNITED STATES: MORTALITY, 2001"

CAUSE OF DEATH BASED ON THE TENTH REVISION,
INTERNATIONAL CLASSIFICATION OF DISEASES

Fire-work

Light Passage—Autumn
Cai Guo-Qiang, 2007

1. 灾

Radical for house. Radical for fire.
    After a last practiced
  Stroke the calligrapher

Into the metal pan passes
    His last scrap of paper.
  Quiet the fall of the paraffin

Light on the library wall,
    The calligrapher's library
  Burns itself down: every scroll

Unscrolls its sallow to the yellow flame,
    The heat unstitches
  Each spine to a spill of pages,

All the loose slips blister into black
    Lace, until that last
  Paper smokes, sizzles its wet ink,

And collapses. The metrical boottaps
    Of the state
  Pass by in the dark street.

Hush here this beautiful catastrophe:
    In the basin's brass
  A bouquet of ash.

2.   滅口

Radical for water, radical for talk.
          The ardent
        Lexicons of the revolution

Blaze on beyond the monastery gate,
                But abandoned, remote,
        Its corridors and dormitories

Murmur the calligrapher's strange exile.
                He keeps the lamps
        Unlit. He keeps himself quiet,

Ghosting the ruined rooms, perusing
                The bare bookshelves
        While on his soundless lips move

Poems no longer bound there. Out on the grounds
                After every rain
        The calligrapher wanders,

With a stick extinguishing each word,
                Stroke by beloved
        Stroke, into the puddles.

3.　花火

At a quick strike on the steel-scratch, the match
　　　　Flares, the fuse catches
　　And crawls in a slow sparkle

To the powderbox propped at the canvas.
　　　　The calligrapher's son
　　Knows his explosives—the blow-

Force of saltpeter, the scatter patterns,
　　　　The weights and burn-rates
　　Of his elements and their velocities,

The hues of their various char against cloth:
　　　　Blueburning copper,
　　Salt red. What is charactered there

In the linen weave is the mind burning
　　　　The thing it loves best
　　To sear its afterimage against

Its forgetting. This is his inheritance,
　　　　This the farewell letter
　　His father never left: radical

For fire and flower together.

Fission

/

Our atomic age: the old marriage
          Gone nuclear,
      The New Mexico summer sear-

Ing through the sheer, unpolarized sky. Wire
          Quaver like a weary
      Choir along the fenceline

Out my son's side window. We have driven
          Beyond the end
      Of everything—roadsigns,

Oiled road, creosote, topograph and color—
          To this scour
      Of hot sand and history.

/

O thou tremble, O omnipotent fleck
　　　　Thou electron!—
　　　Whose testy mysteries at last

Surrender to the lab's dread guesswork.
　　　　Secret and strange,
　　　That a voltage jump should estrange

Such smallness from itself: the atom off-
　　　　Kilter, kinetic
　　　To fracture into spark.

Minutest change, and yet it shudders through
　　　　The testing range
　　　Of the heart. What is there to do

But hunker down and hope the bunker
　　　　We built to shelter
　　　From bigger combustions will hold.

1

And I saw as it were a sea of glass
            Mingled with fire.

/

Speed of light. Speed of more

Than light, of fire's respiring billow
            At the blind
Horizon. The dozen-dozen

Dazzled snap their sunglassed faces skyward,
            But too late: the Lord
Has come and gone, the first flash

An afterimage and a fall of ash.
            Fell and fleet,
Its radiance now commemorate

In cumbrous governmental elements:
            An obelisk
Of rock. A metal plaque.

/

My son has come for the technology.
　　　　　Nerdy and unmoved
　　　He fingers the mortar grooves

As he squats the marker's shade, his palms engraved
　　　　　With the plaque's bland facts
　　　In backward. His foottracks

Map the parameters of mattresses
　　　　　Stacked to catch
　　　The Gadget in some ac-

Cidental drop. The winch might snap, the shot-
　　　　　Tower's top
　　　A hundred vesuvian feet up,

But by God they laid out some mattresses
　　　　　He laughs from inside
　　　His guidebook. The calculus

Of risk and its flimsy solaces is
　　　　　Faith's first and last
　　　Signpost, as his infant sorrow knows

Already. As noons the shadow to its sheer degree
　　　　　His sun-slant hands spell
　　　YTIИIЯT

/

Oppenheimer up all night, his flashlight
　　　　Haloing the barracks
　　　Where he bends across his books,

The sonnets dimly seen. Donne's three-person'd
　　　　God is fading
　　　With the battery, the Bible

On the table open to the Passion's
　　　　Godforsaken.
　　　He has read to the conclusion,

Knows what happens when an elemental
　　　　Whole is put asunder:
　　　Earthquakes. Darkness. Thunder

And a cry. Thus he christens his device:
　　　　Not that God
　　　Shatters us, but that God shatters.

/

Batter **my heart,** three-person'd God; for, you
As yet but knocke, breathe, shine, & **seeke to mend;**
That **I may** rise, and stand, o'erthrow mee,'and **bend**

Your force **to breake**, blowe, burn, & make **me** new.
I, like an usurpt towne, to'another due,
Labour to admit you, but O, to **no** end,

Reason **you**r Viceroy **in me**, me should defend,
But is captiv'd, and **prove**s weake or **untrue,**
Yet **dearly'I love** you, **and would be loved faine,**

But am betroth'd unto your ene**my**:
Divorce me,'untie, or **breake that knot** againe,
Take me **to you,** imprison me,

for I,
Except **you**'en**thrall me, never s**hall be free,

Nor ever chaste, **ex**cept you ravish me**.**

/

I have come for the desert crust in pieces,
        The white-sand surface
     Burnt, blown, broken, and annealed

In green. This valley's chalice once of wrath
        Now full of glints
     As sunlight detonates against

A scattering of trinitite: bright melt
        Of quartz and feld-
     Spar into aquamarine.

By what mystery turn these kilotons
        To crystalline?
     And where that missal can I find

Which Oppenheimer learned?, the one that opens
        The seals of our sorest
     Furies and fuses them

Into a sea of glass?

/

Listen: vested
In my very best
Disaster have I staggered

To this waste, dragging my collateral
Dandling, blasted
Out and on the hustle

For some apocalyptic luster. Let's
Critical some mass.
My mattresses are stacked.

5.12

Hexes. Hooks. Nuts. Full rack of cams.

Quickdraws. Quicklinks.

With what sustaining clanks

They fill the pack, how they heft in the hand

With metallic

Assurance! We palm-fondle,

We fetish with thumbs, we toothbrush off

The grains of sand.

We love the gear as we love

God, as we love any salvation fable,

Believing our love

Hangs from the rope of our peril.

Thus do we sling to an anchor, thus smear

Foot-rubber to rock,

As if every heelhook

And handjam were of faith our testament.

But as any penitent

Knows, it's never grace

That calls us to ascend, but gravity's

Sweet and awful

Hazard. If we weren't in it for the fall,

We'd walk.

Florida

Every beauty barbed, from the tiniest mites
                    Beading the Spanish
          Moss in a drapery of bites

To these dark lawns aquiver with itches.
                    The night buzzes
          And pops like a power surge

Through a fluorescent tube. Unmoving
                    I listen, nightlong
          His body a dear distance

Of sighs beside me. I have married
                    This predation,
          Plighted my troth to its scurry

And sting. I wear like a ring the horizon's
                    Compass of un-
          Familiars: *cormorant*,

Hygrometer, whelk, frangipani.
                    I mouth each strange
          Name as a succulent

Vow to love what I will never tame.
                    Wake, Sweet, and see
          Florida tossing my forever bouquet:

In the hurricane blow from the gulf coast
                    The alligator flag
          Fans its bracts, the ghostpalm ghosts.

FLUID OVERLOAD (E87.7)

WORK TABLE I. DEATHS FROM EACH CAUSE, BY 5-YEAR AGE
GROUPS: UNITED STATES, 2001

All ages --------	68
Under 1 year----	1
1-4 years--------	
5-9 years--------	
10-14 years------	
15-19 years------	
20-24 years------	
25-29 years-----	2
30-34 years-----	1
35-39 years-----	
40-44 years-----	1
45-49 years-----	2
50-54 years-----	1
55-59 years-----	5
60-64 years-----	6
65-69 years-----	8
70-74 years-----	12
75-79 years-----	8
80-84 years-----	16
85-89 years-----	4
90-94 years------	
95-99 years------	
100 yrs & over---	1
Not stated-------	

U.S. ACTUARIAL TABLES/CENTERS FOR DISEASE CONTROL

FOR CAUSE-OF-DEATH CODES, SEE HTTP://WWW.CDC.GOV/NCHS
AND REFER TO "TECHNICAL APPENDIX FROM VITAL STATISTICS
OF THE UNITED STATES: MORTALITY, 2001"

CAUSE OF DEATH BASED ON THE TENTH REVISION,
INTERNATIONAL CLASSIFICATION OF DISEASES

Foley Catheter

I clean its latex length three times a day
           With kindliest touch,
      Swipe an alcohol swatch

From the tender skin at the tip of him
           Down the lumen
      To the drainage bag I change

Each day and flush with vinegar.
           When I vowed *for worse*
      Unwitting did I wed this

Something-other-than-a-husband, jumble
           Of exposed plumbing
      And euphemism. Fumble

I through my nurse's functions, upended
           From the spare bed
      By his every midnight sound.

Unsought inside our grand romantic
           Intimacy
      Another intimacy

Opens, ruthless and indecent, consuming
           All our hiddenmosts.
      In a body, immodest

Such hunger we sometimes call *tumor*;
           In a marriage
      It's *cherish*. From the Latin for *cost*.

Foliate

Rough all day with the reciprocating
Saw, I have hacked at last the branches
From the trunk, axe-bucked everything
To billets. I would rake up and stitch
All these tattered leaves into a letter
I'd send to tell you, Dear One, of the cord
Of kindling stacked against the winter,
The garden box I'll build, the bird-
Houses I'll hang on every vertical,
Swifts and solitaires clustering to my care,
My industry a handsome piece of foil
Behind the brittle glass of what I feared
All along I couldn't save. Shouldn't
That be enough? It should be. But it isn't.

Folio

The king's in rags, the robe of his state unseamed
        Like a flimsy
    Map over- and overfolded.

Finally silent the squabble and scold,
        The family rabble
    Undaughtered by dagger,

By draught and a noose, and his poor fool hanged.
        Never heart
    Had greater cause to quit. The quarto

Stretches Lear upon the world's tough rack
        To sorrow's span
    And then undoes the button

Of his last breath. But the later draft
        Engrafts a father's
    Fancy to his final: *Look there,*

Look there, as if some lively twitch yet flickered
        Upon the lips
    Of the ever-illegible girl.

There at the verge of tragedy, say *Never,*
        Griever, five
    Times over like a fetish,

A fervor of faith that the folio knows
        To deliver
    The one unrecoverable blow:

Come bereave, come bruise, but of all the wounds
We suffer, hope
Will kill us every time.

Font

Hey there, croupier moon—preening your pearl
      Like a cufflink
    Studded in the rucked tuxedo

Of night. I have swerved to your *debonnaire*
      Too often, taken
    My chances with your flair

And your flabbergast of silver in the willows.
      I'm getting wise
    To your sleights, I'm game to throw

Over every gibbous waxing gossamer
      For the dull bulb
    Of tungsten on the table

In the room where my children work their long
      Division.
    I'm louvering down

The shutter's dark, shucking my champagne gown
      For mukluks
    And humdrum; and the hum

Of the night, electric, doesn't buzz
      Through the doors
    I've latched against the flattered

Romance of my own spectacular. I'll forsake
      All that charismatic
    Nonsense in the name of the son

And of the son and of the haloed glow
From that dim lamp
That holds us here as one, for now.

You extravagant, captious, chancy moon,
I renounce you.
I renounce you. I renounce you.

Fontanelle

When you came into the world unfinished
               I mistook you
         For hope. You the wide o-

Pen window in every room, you the flute's
               Embouchure
         To whose new tune the world ever

Puts its breathy mouth. You in spring earth
               The thumbprint
         Into whose keeping I commit

Something scant, something frail to a late frost
               Yet greening
         In tendrils through all that winter lost.

FORMS OF ESSENTIAL TREMOR (G25.0/2)

WORK TABLE I. DEATHS FROM EACH CAUSE, BY 5-YEAR AGE
GROUPS: UNITED STATES, 2001

Age group	Deaths
All ages --------	4
Under 1 year-----	
1-4 years--------	
5-9 years--------	
10-14 years------	
15-19 years------	
20-24 years------	
25-29 years------	
30-34 years------	
35-39 years------	
40-44 years------	
45-49 years------	
50-54 years------	
55-59 years------	
60-64 years------	
65-69 years------	
70-74 years------	1
75-79 years------	
80-84 years------	
85-89 years------	1
90-94 years-----	2
95-99 years------	
100 yrs & over---	
Notstated--------	

U.S. ACTUARIAL TABLES/CENTERS FOR DISEASE CONTROL

FOR CAUSE-OF-DEATH CODES, SEE HTTP://WWW.CDC.GOV/
NCHS AND REFER TO "TECHNICAL APPENDIX FROM VITAL
STATISTICS OF THE UNITED STATES: MORTALITY, 2001"

CAUSE OF DEATH BASED ON THE TENTH REVISION,
INTERNATIONAL CLASSIFICATION OF DISEASES

Formulary

The Adoration of the Mystic Lamb
Hubert and Jan van Eyck, 1432

Hush, lamb, lavish with blood in madder red,
        Your varnish overfed,
     Too fat for this thin season.

Hush, choir—be-rubied, embroidered, unsomber
        As the lute tuned
     To your organ's lustrous umber.

And all you pious press in festal vestments,
        Silken chevaliers
     And saints, fold up your banners,

Fold in your Flemish wings. We must a wan
        And wastrel vista
     Now, at the phlegmatic end

Of spring, swapping our wanton carmines for shamefast
        Grisailles and the stern
     Click of the altarpiece latch.

Here's the catch: though we've stanched our chansons,
        Slouching to matins
     Roughed in our workaday drab,

Yet our grayscales blush under the muffled
        Thrum through the shut
     Hinges like the heat

From a woodstove. We are by beauty shrove,
          And we its pledges
       Confess it in each intemperate

Pulse at the wrist, in the rash prismatics
           Of our glances.
      We've committed its rubrics

To heart. And to all the blackletter
           Austeres
      This our inmost responsory:

Vermillion, crimson, cadmium, madder red.

Foulbrood

A spill of coppers: dead bees scattered
        Across the grass
    From the hive's dropped purse.

In a rotten crotch of my treetrunk humming
        One to one
    To a hundred they bunched

To their hot industry. Honeymouthed, honey-
        Handed they handled
    Nectar to hexagons,

The broody queen bustling by chambers her much-
        Motherly fuss.
    Tucked in a covert of bark

The bulge of it filled in a fortnight, banked
        And excitable
    As a circuit box. Better

A live wire snapping its spark and writhe
        Than this collapse—
    The hive and all its hopes

Undone. Under a dinless noon, the bee-bodies
        Keep their secrets:
    What sly menace breached

Their stingered care and struck the colony down,
How they could bear
Their careful, consuming

Tenderness, knowing the risk.

Freefall

Dearly beloved, how headlong the pledge

Of the jump:

The open, implacable hatch,

Propeller's hot wash thumping like a heart

In the ear,

Toetips pivoting over

The last row of rivets to pitch

Into air! air!

Fathoms of air!, the King Air

Plummeting upward from my body's absurd

Downward

Majesty, my oath

To gravity attested in this

My breakable

Flesh. As breathless

It blurs toward the resolute ground,

The sky sudden

Jerks, opens, silken

Into crimson, a poppy in the button-

Hole of day.

Another pops some yards away

And then another, bright receiving line

Curtseying

Its gracious welcome down

The middle atmosphere. What betrayal

To find

After my flamboyant fall

I favor this buoyant parachute drift—

The wedding

Party to the wedding.

Groom of earth, if you want to embrace me,

You must marry me

More quickly, more quickly.

Frescoes

Davit Gareji, 9th–13th C.

The convent keeps its sacrament of rock,
      A pick-and-chisel
    Consecration, every cell

One station of a holy isolation.
      To this fastness
    Have I brought my byzantine

Fixation on all things monastic, born
      Of a notion
    That silent and withdrawn

I might at last enclose my fugitive
      Virtue in a bare,
    Bored heart. But every chamber

A debauch of color: Christ of ochre
      Slouching one saucy
    Thigh askance; velvet-cloaked

Christ with red lips asimper and the sad
      Orthodox
    Eyes of a lover. I have betrayed

My dun ascetic from my earliest,
      Beneath the burlap
    Of my swaddling I have pulsed

Into my very plaster, cinnabar
        Blush down to the rough
    Of my bones, and no chantry far

Or flint enough to unfix it. God knows we bear
        Our truest cloister
    With us as we go.

Frogs

Four poets in the Alps. How hackled we
                    At the Romantic
                    Cliché we cut, the twee

Shelleyan swoon of it all, how antsy
                    To cast our clever
                    To the counterstance: no pensées

Hackneying every wistful vista, no
                    Firelight's earnest
                    Flickering on our late philo-

Sophy. Under a droll umber of tourism
                    Someone found
                    Our fittest excursion, museum

Of napoleonic frogs, a hundred
                    Posed in daily scenes:
                    At school, at billiards, girded

For battle with some dread but tardy foe.
                    Fatigued by war,
                    Infirm, the former officer

Foraged for frogs across his sodden farmland,
                    Hauling them home
                    By the canvas bagful, by hand

Fondly scooped he their guts out their mouths,
                    Filled their hollows
                    With sand and arranged dioramas,

Mascots of our wry postmodern travels.
But Jay unraveled,
Veering between choler

And despair, his chemo drug's distemper;
Meg brooded on
The ambush in her breastbone,

Her treason cells combusting once again
In malign fractals;
Josh spurned his impish muse to spoon

Up against his mortal day, just the one snuff
To his name
But resolute as fuck to poem

It first. And I,—I too exhausted
From attending
The unhurried deaths of my beloveds

To make the drive, and Estavayer-le-Lac
Seemed so, so far—
I unironic watched the weather

Turn against the terrible peaks, gothic
And aloof, cold
Testament to the visible world.

As nightly from the stripped cathedrals poured
Bells their dour
Calvinist admonishments

We four tableau-vivanted Switzerland,
    Souls emptied
Through our mouths and filled with sand.

Fulminate

I saw you coming from a mile away,
        Thunder. You play
     Coy, sly your pretty in winks

Around the cloudbank, but up close what colors
        You show, all shazam
     And tantrum while the *Wham-bam*

On the wireless crackles with static. What the swagger
        Are you after?,
     Whose the heart you do not stagger

When you rattle through the bracken, knocking
        Branches at the casement?
     I betook me to the basement

When you batted first your lashes, flashed
        Me your distant
     Dazzle—I've been whiplashed

By your type before: you come on easy
        But want me on my knees,
     Want to flutter my transformers

And shut off all my lights. You throw a glam show
        And then you blow
     Along to the next hapless,

Leaving blank fuzz across the radio dial—
        No tune, no storm-
     Warning, no *Thank you ma'am.*

Fumarole

Beyond the spelunker's last chossy handfast,

    Past the furthest

        Unwind of a rescuer's line,

A boy as limber and scabbed as I

    Got him wedged tight

        In a pinch of granite.

I have finger-and-toed that hole, forward

    Inch by inch, cheek

        By rock, have jackknifed my hipsockets

Over the jut that caught him up, have fumbled

    Fingerblind

        For an edge, an elbow for leverage,

A pull and then through. What I found down

    In that hot dark

        I've forgotten. The ground

Is an oubliette wherein unechoed, dull,

      The tongue unsings

           Its hungers, and the human

Push to prove itself runs out against

      The terminal

           Wall, breathless and bent small.

Whatever the boy found belongs now

      To cement and trowel.

           They sealed the cave's mouth when he died.

FUNCTIONAL DISORDER, UNSPECIFIED (K59.9)

WORK TABLE I. DEATHS FROM EACH CAUSE, BY 5-YEAR AGE
GROUPS: UNITED STATES, 2001

```
All ages --------      25
Under 1 year-----       1
1-4 years--------
5-9 years--------
10-14 years------
15-19 years------       1
20-24 years------
25-29 years------
30-34 years------
35-39 years------
40-44 years------
45-49 years------
50-54 years------
55-59 years------
60-64 years------       2
65-69 years------       2
70-74 years------       2
75-79 years------       5
80-84 years------       5
85-89 years------       4
90-94 years------       3
95-99 years------
100 yrs & over---
Not stated-------
```

U.S. ACTUARIAL TABLES/CENTERS FOR DISEASE CONTROL

FOR CAUSE-OF-DEATH CODES, SEE HTTP://WWW.CDC.GOV/NCHS
AND REFER TO "TECHNICAL APPENDIX FROM VITAL STATISTICS
OF THE UNITED STATES: MORTALITY, 2001"

CAUSE OF DEATH BASED ON THE TENTH REVISION,
INTERNATIONAL CLASSIFICATION OF DISEASES

Funerals

There was the one we planned in the parking
           Lot, gearshift forgot
       In neutral, motor overhot, stunned sunset

Blinding off the diagnostic complex.
               The one from behind
       The radiation lead, his hand

Snuck out to my protected plastic chair
           Listing finger
       To finger his favorite hymns.

The one in the dim drip of the chemo
               Ward, the onco
       Nurses shushing our too-raucous

List of uninvites. The heavy art
               Of giving grief
       Some wieldy order finds relief

In much revising, its gravity leavened
               To a new genre.
       Even grief itself softens,

Unbarbing as each black dress falls out
               Of fashion,
       As each floral spray's carnations

Brown and curl, as every evening adds
               Its soft amen
       To this protracted requiem.

But in all the breviaries, in the dirges,
           In the obituary pages
           And the eulogies of strangers,

There is no form for what I have become,
           Half-widowèd
           So long before my widowhead:

Unhusbanded. Unfutured. Uncondoled.
           Under the dull
           Hospital fluorescence a pall

Settles, tender and indiscriminate;
           Into its keeping
           I my everything commit.

Fusion

Goddamn my quantum soul—restive, sizzling
        In its nimbus
      Of need. How it dizzies

In the orbit of another's passing
        Fancy, fickle
      As it flirts its vacant shells

Hey there sexy fella can you fill
        My spinning empties
      With your any loose electrons?,

How in relentless ciphers it scrawls
        On any bathroom wall
      My atomic number.

It is a light element, an errant
        Sphere with strong wants:
      Come Lover, let's charge ourselves

A spark, a star, a dark and secret
        Supernova, let
      Us cleave ourselves: attract,

Repel, attract, repel, and let us fall
        In common gravity,
      By which I mean love, and then fall-

Out.

Fuschia

You can play the actuary,

Index threats by alphabet, unthreat
            Their jolts and pricks
        With civil statistics

In columns. So many the flesh's affronts:
            The canker
        Whose black obduracy festers

In your love's skeleton, the gnawed bone
            Of divorce
        Still sharp with splinters

All these years on, the untimely pall
            Settling spectral
        Across your mother's features.

You can file and sort. You can classify,
            A librarian
        Shelving the ephemera—

Diagnoses and quitclaims, foreclosures and bonds—
            Under F (*Very*
        Local American History),

One event succeeding to the next
            As a prodigy
        Of logic. But then: a flight

Of finches lifts sudden off the fenceline,
A leafwing clings
Spotlit against the kitchen screen,

A thunderous sunset glooms into a color
You last saw
In an April meadow

The wind was thrashing into
A glossolalia,
And at once your long

And heedful business toward order
Collapses
Under the weight of joy.

F-word

How foolish I for fretting after silver
Linings, as if loss were not the principle
Of love. From its first resistless quiver
The heart keeps giving its stupid all,
That fleshy bankrupt, to what beloved ever
It sets itself upon. You are dear, Dear
One, because of the expense—in fear,
In wakefulness, in all the unrecover-
Able tenders that account my faith.
I am in forfeiture, and nothing worth
But what unthrift I freely risk in you,
You my Hesperides, unguarded gold
Orchard at the danger edge of the world.

Notes

In 2001, my first child was born; suddenly, the whole world seemed fatal. The actuarial tables interspersed throughout the text come from the Centers for Disease Control's 2001 report on mortality from all causes: https://www.cdc.gov/nchs/data/statab/mortfinal2001_worki.pdf.

"F-hole" owes its life to the study "The evolution of air resonance power efficiency in the violin and its ancestors," by Hadi T. Nia, Ankita D. Jain, Yuming Liu, Mohammad-Reza Alam, Roman Barnas, and Nicholas C. Makris (Royal Society, 2015).

"Fire-work": Section 1's 灾 is a calligraphic character that means "disaster"; the pictogram from which it derives signifies a fire in a house. Section 2 begins with two characters that come together to mean "to silence someone": 滅口; the term's first character contains the water radical and means "to extinguish or put out," and the second character means "mouth or speech." The characters that begin the poem's third section, 花火, mean "flower" and "fire," respectively; together, they signify "fireworks." I am grateful to M. Alexander Turner for his generous help with Chinese vocabulary and characters. The calligrapher is the father of firework artist Cai Guo-Qiang, and the story of his perilous love for his manuscripts is related in the profile "Meet the Artist Who Blows Things Up for a Living," by Ron Rosenbaum, in the April 2013 issue of *Smithsonian*.

"Folio": The early text of William Shakespeare's *King Lear* existed in two very different versions, the Quarto of 1608 and the Folio of 1623. In the Folio version, Lear dies seeming to believe that Cordelia is reviving.

"Formulary" is for Mary Szybist.

"Frogs," which refers to the amphibian dioramas at the Museum Estavayer-le-Lac et ses grenouilles, is for Josh Bell.

"Frescoes": Endless thanks to Natasha Lomouri and Manana Matiashvili for Georgian guidance and hospitality.

"Fulminate" quotes David Bowie, "Suffragette City," from the album *The Rise and Fall of Ziggy Stardust and the Spiders from Mars* (RCA, 1972).

"Fumarole": On November 24, 2009, John Edward Jones died after having been trapped upside-down in Nutty Putty Cave, in the Utah desert, for 28 hours.

"Fuschia": The Library of Congress classification system designates "Local History of the Americas" as call sign F.

The three sonnets are for Meg Day.

Acknowledgments

I gratefully recognize the following publications, in which some of these poems, occasionally in different form, first appeared.

Boulevard, The Cincinnati Review, Crazyhorse, Gettysburg Review, Harvard Review, Kenyon Review, New England Review, New Ohio Review, New Orleans Review, Plume, Poetry International, Poetry Northwest, Prairie Schooner, Sewanee Review, Western Humanities Review.

*

"Farrow" and "Foley Catheter" appeared as part of the Academy of American Poets Poem-A-Day series.

"Farrow" appeared in *The Orison Anthology*, volume 1, edited by Luke Hankins, Nathan Poole, and Karen Tucker (Asheville NC: Orison Press, 2016).

"Farthingale" appeared on *Verse Daily*.

"Farthingale" and "Freefall" appeared in *The Helicon West Anthology*, edited by Star Coulbrooke, Tim Keller, and Chadd VanZanten (Logan UT: Helicon West Press, 2016).

"Female" appeared in *Women of Resistance: Poems for a New Feminism*, edited by Danielle Barnhart and Iris Mahan (New York: OR Books, 2018).

"Female," "Folio," and "Formulary" appeared on *Poetry Daily*.

"F-hole" appeared in *The Eloquent Poem*, edited by Elise Paschen (New York NY: Persea Books, 2019).

"Fifteen" appeared in *The Best American Poetry 2020*, edited by Paisley Rekdal (New York NY: Scribner, 2020).

"Fumarole" appeared in *Utah@125*, a digital chapbook celebrating 125 years of Utah's statehood (https://thrive125.utah.gov/utah-at-125).

*

Praises to Linda Gregerson, whose supple tercet shaped my shifting rhyme.

Enduring thanks to my attentive editor Gabriel Fried, and to all at Persea Books for supporting my work from the first.

Gratitude to Jay Hopler for being my first and last reader and my tuning fork, and for endowing the Solitude Nordic Center Writing Retreat year upon year. Love as ever to Elijah and Bennett, and to the whole fam. Meg, Chelsea, and Frankie are forever my kin 🤟. Riley Lorimer has a very welcome habit of stepping in to save the day. Josh Bell, Lisa Bickmore, Melissa Range, and Paisley Rekdal read versions of this book in draft form and provided crucial feedback. I am rescued regularly by the good words and good care of Simon Browne, Jim Galvin, Mark Halliday, Kristin Matthews, Jill McDonough, and the limerick bosses of the John Donne Society. Thanks to Natasha Sajé, Susan Sample, and Jennifer Tonge for nourishing me, body and mind. This book's primary companions of the ear were David Mead and Frightened Rabbit.